W9-BIF-417

101
EDUCATIONAL

VITO PERRONE
Teaching, Curriculum, and
Learning Environments Chair
at HARVARD UNIVERSITY

CHELSEA HOUSE PUBLISHERS
New York • Philadelphia

CONVERSATIONS

With Your 3rd Grader

First Printing

1 3 5 7 9 8 6 4 2

Library of Congress Cataloging-in-Publication Data

Perrone, Vito.
  101 educational conversations to have with your child / Vito Perrone
p. cm.
  Includes bibliographical references and index.
  ISBN 0-7910-1919-5
      0-7910-1984-5 (pbk.)
  1. Education—United States—Parent participation. 2. Third grade (Education)—United States. 3. Parent and child—United States. 4. Communication—United States. I. Title. II. Title: One hundred one educational conversations with your third grader. III. Title: One hundred and one educational conversations with your third grader. IV. Series: Perrone, Vito. 101 educational conversations you should have with your child.
LB1048.5.P46 1993   92-28529
370.19'31—dc20   CIP

Cover photo: Addie Passen

CONTENTS

Unlike most countries, the United States does not have a formal national curriculum. In theory, each of the 15,000 school districts in the United States creates—with direction from state education agencies—its own curriculum. In practice, however, there are more similarities than differences among these curricula. What amounts to a national curriculum has been created through years of curriculum development by various national organizations related to the various subject areas, through the widespread use of textbooks prepared for a national market, and through standardized testing programs that are national in scope and are designed that the performance of children in any grade can be compared to the performance of children in the same grade but in a different community or state.

As a result of these standardizing forces, children in North Dakota study much the same subjects in their social studies classes, for example, as students in Massachusetts and Washington. They study their neighborhoods in grades 1 and 2, their cities in grade 3, their states in grade 4, American history in grade 5, some form of world history in grade 6, Latin America and Canada in grade 7, American history in grade 8, civics or world history in grade 9, global history or American history in grade 10, American history in grade 11, and either American government and economics or an elective course in American history or world history in grade 12.

The science curriculum becomes somewhat standardized in grade 9 with the study of physical science or earth science. High school students study biology in grade 10, chemistry in grade 11, and either physics or an elective course in biology or physical science in grade 12. In mathematics they study algebra I in grade 9, geometry in grade 10, algebra II in grade 11, and either trigonometry and precalculus or calculus in grade 12.

Each volume in the *101 Educational Conversations You Should Have with Your Child* series contains an outline of the typical curriculum for that particular grade. But you will probably find it helpful to ask your child's teacher about the curriculum for each new grade your child enters. The teacher can give you a fuller account of what is being taught in your school system.

You and Your Child's Education

Welcome to *101 Educational Conversations with Your Third Grader,* one of a series of books for parents who wish to be more involved in their children's education. I have written these books with two important goals in mind—first, to give parents a solid basis for talking with their children about their school experiences and thereby gaining further insight into their children's growth as learners; and second, to guide parents toward constructive, education-oriented interaction with teachers and administrators in their children's schools.

In my 30 years of experience in and around schools, I have found that parents are not always clear about what their children are learning in school, about whether their children's overall education is powerful or trivial, challenging or dull. Furthermore, parents often lack a vision of what the schools—at their best—should provide students. We must acknowledge, of course, that not all of what children must ultimately know and understand is learned in the schools. However, the schools do have an intentional curriculum, regardless of the grade level.

In the early years, schools expect to teach children reading and writing, as well as certain aspects of science, social studies, and mathematics. They also expect to introduce children to the arts. These efforts should enable children not only to build upon what they learn at home but also to extend their classroom learning into the world outside school. Parents are a vital part of this endeavor. The more you know about the school's intentions and your child's responses, the better for your child's overall education.

Parents invariably ask their children, "What did you learn (or do) at school today?" and are treated to what has become the classic, predictable response: "Nothing." This is clearly a discouraging exchange, leaving parents on the outside or making them feel that they must press their children for details. But a parent's insistence only makes the exchange rather unnatural or even negative, with problematic results. Not only does the parent gain few new insights into the child's education, but the child may come to resent what he or she perceives as a grilling or as a routine, meaningless inquiry. The *101 Educational Conversations You Should Have with Your Child* series is designed to help parents get closer to what their children are learning. It encourages parents to find out what their children understand and also what they do not yet understand. The goal is to make parents' exchanges with their children about school and learning more natural and enjoyable, a mutual treat rather than a mutual burden.

At various times in the school year, parents are invited to parent-teacher conferences, where they often hear a good deal about their children's progress in different subjects. In most cases, however, parents bring too little to these meetings. Rather than being genuine conversations, the conferences are one-sided reports. Parents may leave these sessions satisfied enough, though in my experience few of them say that they are fully engaged by the process. The *101 Educational Conversations You Should Have with Your Child* series should contribute to constructive change. These books are tools with which you can inform yourself about what the schools hope to teach and what your children are learning. You should then be able to bring to the parent-teacher conferences some of your own insights and perspectives about your children's educational growth. You will also be able to pose more potent questions to your children's teachers. As a result, your interactions with teachers should become more interesting and more constructive. The children and the schools will surely benefit.

An important premise of this series is that parents are their children's *first* teachers and their most critically important partners in learning. While this may seem most obvious to parents when their children are in the early primary grades, it is vital for parents to remain involved throughout their children's school lives. This is not, I grant, always easy. For one thing, parents often do not really know what the schools are teaching. In this regard the schools should be expected to provide much better information. Weekly guides would not be too much to expect. Nor would occasional workshops to give parents a fuller understanding of the questions children are asked in school, the books children read, and the principal objectives of the curriculum. If the schools do not deliver this kind of information to parents, then parents should ask, Why not?

Further, while schools typically say they value parent participation, parents are not always treated as full partners. This must change. If the schools do not actively acknowledge and encourage a strong role for parents, then parents themselves should take the initiative. Although this book is most concerned with the parent-child exchange, it will not have succeeded if it does not also empower parents in their relationships with their children's schools and teachers. In the end, the educational partnerships that we so desperately need—between parents and their children and between parents and schools—will be stronger.

101 Educational Conversations with Your Third Grader focuses on three areas of interest to parents:

- An overview of the third grade, with a look at how classrooms are organized, the kinds of experiences that are offered to children in school, and the basic curriculum—the content of what is taught.

- A collection of conversation starters and suggested activities— a how-to guide for parents who want to explore and expand their children's learning process through creative, stress-free interactions.

- A parent's guide to interacting with teachers and school administrators.

I wish to make one last point in this introduction. In the course of a school year, children study across many fields of inquiry. They read numerous books, view large numbers of films and videos, respond to many hundreds of questions, hear about a myriad of individuals and groups, explore the geography and politics of many countries, and learn many small facts and some larger conceptions. This book, and the others in this series, cannot cover *all* the ground that a child covers in a year. The most it can offer is a variety of useful places to begin. I expect that, once given these important guideposts, parents will be able to develop their own conversations and activities to enhance their understanding of their children's education while in turn enlarging the educational possibilities for the children. I trust that all of you who read this and the other books in the *101 Educational Conversations You Should Have with Your Child* series will have as good a time using the ideas as I and my colleagues have had in putting them together.

1
Your Child's Classroom

The best third grade classrooms are *developmentally appropriate*. This means that most activities are based on the physical, intellectual, social, and emotional development of each child, *not* on the children's ages or grade levels. Some third grade children, for example, are very independent readers; others are still working on a variety of reading skills and consolidating their mastery of reading. Expecting all children to be at the same point, and teaching as if they were, not only limits the learning experience for many children but for some children induces feelings of failure that will not easily be overcome. Attention to individual development rather than emphasis on grade levels is very important.

Developmentally appropriate classrooms are characterized by certain features. Among the most important of these are:

Respect for the Children

- Children's interests are important starting points for learning.

- Children's ideas and work are taken seriously.

- Children are understood to be actively in search of knowledge. Their play, questions, constructions, and speech are seen as part of the process of building knowledge.

- Children do as much talking as the teachers.

- Children have many opportunities to choose—the literature they read, the projects they do, the activities they participate in.

- Children have *time* to look around, wonder, and dream.

- Children work cooperatively, helping each other.

- Individual, racial, linguistic, and cultural differences are celebrated. They are seen as ways of enriching the children's lives.

Stimulation of Thought, Imagination, and Self-esteem

- As children move beyond information to understanding, teachers respond to children's ideas and questions in ways that extend their learning rather than with rote answers.

- Teachers (and children) ask more open-ended questions than yes-or-no questions. Teachers spark exchanges by saying, "What if we did it this way?" "How else could we do it?" "Who has thought of another way?" "Is there another viewpoint?"

- Considerable attention is given to the processes of exploration and discovery, inquiry and investigation.

- Errors are seen as steps toward further learning, as particular inventions—not as mistakes or failures. Teachers respond to errors in ways that keep children's self-esteem intact and leave them eager to learn, not fearful of making mistakes.

- Teachers encourage risk taking and provide a safe, supportive environment for it.

An Abundance of Chances To Learn

- All forms of communication are given attention: reading, writing, listening, speaking. The classroom is full of language.

- The classroom is inviting and colorful, with a variety of interesting materials. The children know where these materials are kept and how to use them.

- Although third grade children's learning activities rely more upon texts than was the case in the earlier grades, real experiences, concrete materials, and hands-on activities are still important. Teachers help the children make connections between the various areas of study. Knowledge is presented as an interconnected web, not as a handful of distinct categories that are unrelated to each other.

- Teachers keep learning, and they share what they learn with their students. They demonstrate that learning is a lifelong process and a source of delight.

- Children write their own books, which in turn can be read by others in the class. Moreover, notes, letters, information, poems, and song lyrics are highly visible in the classroom.

- Children read real books by real authors, not just committee-produced "readers."

- Teachers know that learning takes place over time, and that children need numerous and related experiences before they are able to absorb critical concepts and use these concepts effectively as the basis of new learning.

- Evidence of interest in science and mathematics is highly visible.

Opportunities for Self-expression and Connections to the Children's Life Outside School

- Children have daily opportunities to participate in the creative and expressive arts: music, drawing, storytelling, drama.

- Children have daily opportunities to run, jump, climb, and play organized games. Physical activities are seen as important for health as well as for building self-confidence.

- Parents are welcome in the classroom. They are encouraged to be active participants in their children's education.

- Teachers make an effort to connect children's lives in school to experiences outside of school such as reading at home, getting a pet, taking a family vacation, eating a new food for the first time, seeing a movie with their parents, and the like.

Teachers who think in developmental terms understand that they can return often to a particular topic of study. Each time they do so, the children's levels of comprehension will have changed. I know of one child who, after reading a story about ice cream, told his teacher that he thought ice cream could be made by pouring milk into a glass of ice cubes and waiting for the ice cubes to melt. Rather than simply telling the boy that this was not true, she suggested that he try it at home and see what happened. He came to school the next day and told the teacher that the milk had gotten very cold—but it was not what he would call ice cream. She then gave him a recipe for ice cream and promised that the class would make some together. Most third grade children would have quickly dismissed the notion of milk turning into ice cream in a glass. Understanding that this child was at a different level of comprehension, however, the teacher respected the child's idea, encouraged him to test it, and then guided him toward more accurate information.

A teacher might ask children to sort rocks into different piles according to how the rocks look to them. A few third grade children will sort the rocks into only two piles: big and small, perhaps, or dark and light. Most children, though, will be able to sort the rocks into more piles, adding such variables as shape, surface texture, and weight. And by grade 4, all children will be able to work with several attributes at once. The concrete experiences along the way make a difference, as do the opportunities to have conversations about what they are doing.

In developmental classrooms, teachers often build the curriculum around themes. For instance, the children may be studying traditional West African masks. They will read about the masks and their place in the cultures of West Africa. And they will make papier-mâché masks, developing designs in the West African style and painting the masks according to these designs. In the process they will learn about the original sources of the paints used in West Africa. Finally they will perform traditional dramas and dances with the masks. Their study of masks will have integrated reading, social studies, and the arts.

The Physical Environment

What are third grade classrooms like? At their best they are more decentralized than organized into a single pattern. They should have many diverse spaces organized for a variety of purposes. Instead of desks they often contain small moveable tables and chairs that can easily be arranged and rearranged. In settings without desks each child will have a space, usually a box (or cubby), for his or her important belongings. These spaces are treated with great respect by the teachers and the children.

While teachers will organize the various learning spaces in their classrooms according to their own preferences, the arrangements described below are not uncommon in classrooms from kindergarten through third grade.

READING

The reading area is particularly inviting. It is brightly carpeted, with pillows on the floor or chairs for students to sit on, and with many books and magazines that are freely accessible to the children. The reading materials cover a broad range of subjects and encompass a broad range of ability and interest levels. Among them are quite a few books written by the children themselves. On display are "ideas for sharing," "new books in the center," and "books I especially liked." Such descriptions are written by the children as well as by the teacher. (In addition to the reading area in the classroom, a third grade class will make considerable use of the school's main library.)

LANGUAGE ARTS

The language arts area, next to the reading area, contains materials and equipment relating to the whole spectrum of communications: pencils and paper, a typewriter, several computers and a printer, a tape recorder with headsets, and a variety of tapes. Some of the tapes are different kinds of music for the children's enjoyment; others are recordings of fiction, biographies, and famous speeches; still others provide skill lessons, such as ways of choosing topics to write about or instructions for doing science projects. There is also a variety of puzzles and a box containing pictures and ideas for writing. Poetry and stories created by the children are displayed in this area of the classroom.

SCIENCE

The science area is designed for active involvement with materials. It changes more often than most of the other learning centers in the room, and it generally contains more "common," noncommercial materials than the other centers. A variety of units from the Elementary Science Study ("small things," "peas and particles," "structures," "pendulums") are found here. These are open-ended study tools that give children experience in such processes as analyzing, classifying, measuring, and predicting. They employ balances, lenses, simple microscopes, magnets, prisms, thermometers, plastic tubing, bottles and jugs, containers with water and sand, candles, rocks, and shells. There might also be an incubator, small motors, nuts and bolts, and pulleys. And there will often be living things: an aquarium with a variety of water life and cages with hamsters. It is also likely that an electric frying pan will be available at least once a week for cooking projects. (Cooking produces enormous enthusiasm because everyone can be successful at it. In addition, it provides an excellent opportunity for integrating the various curriculum areas; in the course of planning a cooking project and following a recipe, children work with concepts from science, health, reading, and math.) The science area will also hold primary science reference books on animals, plants, insects, rocks, astronomy, and engines. Projects that have been completed by individuals or groups of children are on display.

MATH

The math area stresses both thinking and active involvement with materials. Activities such as measuring, weighing, graphing, sorting, and classifying are encouraged. Tools to help children with these activities are at hand—including tape measures, string, rulers, balances, and jars of various sizes. There are also plenty of things to help children count and learn about geometric shapes: abacuses, dice, Cuisenaire rods, multicolored and multishaped blocks, and tangrams (Chinese puzzles with geometric shapes that can be put together in a variety of ways). There are math games and puzzles, along with "activity cards" that guide children toward sequential learning of some mathematical concepts, helping them see patterns and relationships.

ART

The art area contains several easels; together they can serve six to eight children. The area also contains such art supplies as aprons, paints (water and tempera), jars, brushes, many different kinds of paper, clay, chalk, scissors, and a variety of craft materials such as egg cartons, glue, string, vinyl tile, wood chips, yarn, wallpaper, and magazines. At times, because of the children's interests or activities, the art area also contains leaves, starch, Styrofoam, rubber, twigs, dyes, and looms.

WOODWORKING

The woodworking area includes an old table that serves as a workbench. Hammers, saws, screwdrivers, pliers, nails, rulers, glue, wire, and sandpaper are stored on a pegboard or in plastic containers. Local lumberyards supply scraps of wood from which the children make boxes, boats, rockets, and geometric designs.

A classroom should be a rich environment with a wide range of learning materials—paints, brushes, wood, paper, books, scissors, batteries, masking tape, wire, audio tapes, filmstrips, and more. The teacher will consider it important that the children know what materials are available, where they are stored, and how to use them. By this point in their school lives, most of the children have learned how to use the tools and equipment safely, and they have virtually complete access to all materials. The teacher knows that if children do not know what is available to them, or if they must ask permission to use the items (which usually involves waiting), they may lose interest, and their opportunities for exploration will be limited. It should be noted, too, that children in such a classroom do things for themselves: they mix paints and clean brushes, and they operate tape recorders, filmstrip projectors, record players, and computers. These simple tasks are part of the process of learning self-reliance and responsibility.

2 What Parents Want To Know

Parents of primary school children often ask how large or small the class should be. Class size *is* important. Ideally, a third grade classroom should have no more than 18 to 22 children. Because children's levels of learning vary widely throughout the early school years, the more individual attention teachers can provide, and the more experiences they can facilitate for each child, the better. But as class size goes beyond 22 students, the potential for individual interaction decreases.

In the previous chapter, I explained the importance of having an abundance of varied learning materials in the classroom. My experience is that as class size reaches 24, 28, or 30 children—which is too often the norm—the classroom becomes a less rich environment for each child. Teachers and parents need to become more vocal about the importance of class size in these early, most formative years.

Another question that comes up often is, How much homework is reasonable for third grade children? Most teachers do not assign much formal homework during the early years, but *some* homework could be useful, especially if it is interesting, if it goes beyond the daily school activities, and if it can be done with a parent.

Homework assignments in the third grade might include: Read your new story to your mother or father. Measure the doors or windows in your house. Read for 20 minutes on your own. Think about words related to outer space, or mountains, or agriculture. Write a story. Watch a particular program on television and note the number of men and women who appear in it. A third grader might also be expected to complete some mathematics problems, or to collect dandelions for a science experiment. But third grade children should *not* have homework that takes more than 30 to 40 minutes. If their homework assignments regularly exceed this limit, parents should inquire about it. And if there is *no* homework, that too is worth an inquiry.

I am often asked about the use of computers. Many children today use computers at home at age five or six, and a growing number of schools have installed computers in primary grade classrooms. Much can be done with computers, especially in word processing, mathematics, and problem-solving exercises. Third grade is a good time for children to become familiar with the computer and begin using it regularly. Keyboarding may at first pose a challenge, but by the end of third grade children should be reasonably skilled in entering words, sentences, paragraphs, and commands.

A Parent's Guide to Teachers' Terminology

As they become involved with their children's schools, parents will hear teachers use many special terms to describe what happens in the classroom. Some of the most important terms are explained below.

LEARNING STYLES
Children learn in many different ways, although each child has a preference for one or two particular ways of learning. These preferen-

ces are called *learning styles*. Some children learn most easily when ideas, concepts, and information are first presented visually, through pictures or videos. Others gain understanding only after firsthand work such as writing, experimenting, problem solving, or play-acting. Some children need to have ideas presented in a very precise and sequential order; for others, close attention to sequence complicates learning rather than promoting it. Teachers are most effective when they know children well enough to understand their individual learning styles. This lets them individualize each child's learning experiences.

INVENTIVE OR TRANSITIONAL SPELLING

Teachers typically get children started writing in kindergarten. By third grade children should be writing every day. Parents will notice that their children are, for the most part, using conventional "correct" spelling. But teachers will still encourage children to use inventive spellings—their own constructs—for words that they do not yet know how to spell. "The hors is wrking" (the horse is working) is a satisfactory piece of *early* writing for some children, as the teacher's primary goal is to keep them writing. By the end of the third grade, however, most children are well along in conventional spelling. But pushing them there too soon will likely diminish them as writers.

BASAL READERS

Basal readers are textbooks designed to teach reading in a sequential, skill-oriented way. They are generally accompanied by numerous prepackaged materials, including workbooks. The stories included in the basal readers have controlled vocabularies, progressing from what are viewed as easier words to more complex words, from very short sentences of three words to longer sentences of four to six words, and the like. Most schools use basal readers, although if they are rigidly followed they do not match the principles of developmentally appropriate classrooms.

Some children, for example, need much more experience with language—hearing more language in more contexts, talking more, seeing more printed letters and words—before they can effectively move forward in the basal reading series. But the basal program assumes that all children of the same age start from the same point. Because everything in the program is sequential, those who have less language experience when they start the program tend to stay behind as readers. Young children do not need this kind of negative experience with reading. On the other hand, for those who are very independent readers, the basal program may provide little challenge.

LITERATURE-BASED READING PROGRAMS

Literature-based reading programs, often called "whole language programs," take a different approach to reading than do the basals. In a literature-based program, children read books by identified authors—books such as Beatrix Potter's *Peter Rabbit*, Mary Hoffman's *Amazing Grace*, and Madeleine L'Engle's *A Wrinkle in Time*. A classroom using this approach to reading will have many books of all kinds, on a variety of topics, at many levels of complexity. Some of these books will be relatively easy to read, others more difficult. The children make choices about which books they read. A growing number of teachers believe that literature-based reading programs are not only more appropriate developmentally than skill-based basal reading programs but help the children become more effective as readers and writers.

PHONICS

Phonics is a system of teaching children to read by sounding out individual letters. For example, a child might read the word *book* by sounding out the *b*, the *oo*, and the *k*: "buh," "oo," "kuh"—"book." The role of phonics in reading programs has become a subject of highly charged debate. Proponents of phonics argue that it is the key to reading; others suggest that it bears little important relationship to reading and wastes children's time. I do not view phonics as an either-or proposition. Many children—but not all of them—are likely to benefit from some attention to phonics. It will be useful to them to know how to use sounds as a way to deal with unfamiliar words, although they should also be encouraged to try other methods of approaching new words, such as the context in which the word appears or its similarity to other words. Regardless of the method they use to teach reading, the most effective teachers will introduce phonics quite naturally within the context of their work with language, even as they understand that turning phonics into a separate activity is not a particularly constructive use of time. Attention to phonics will cease by the end of third grade.

DISCOVERY LEARNING

In classrooms organized around discovery learning, children are encouraged to ask questions, investigate subjects that interest them, and find solutions to problems. Teachers tend not to provide answers but rather to help children seek their own answers. Teachers encourage questions by raising questions themselves, by filling the classrooms with interesting materials, and by drawing upon many of the children's own experiences.

Suppose a child wants to know more about a particular city—Boston, for example. The teacher might ask the child what ideas he or she already has about finding the information and then suggest additional avenues for exploration. The conversation might go like this:

TEACHER: How could you find out more about Boston?

CHILD: Read, look in the encyclopedia or a book about cities, find it on a map, ask my mom.

TEACHER: If you used the map, what would you expect to learn?

CHILD: I'm not sure.

TEACHER: Let's look at a map together and see what information it provides about Boston.

Here is another example of the kind of exchange that is heard in discovery-based classrooms:

TEACHER: How would you know how many balls it would take to fill up this cylinder?

CHILD: Let's fill the cylinder with the balls and count them.

TEACHER: That is one way. Let's do that, but then let's see if we can figure out any other ways.

The teacher's role in the discovery-based classroom is to help children find many of their own solutions by giving them a framework for asking and answering questions. Essentially, the teacher introduces children to new ways of thinking.

COOPERATIVE LEARNING

Cooperative learning is a means of helping children work together in order to increase their learning. Cooperative learning groups are organized to allow students to work on projects together, solve mathematics and science problems, do experiments, share stories, read to each other, and the like. In the third grade, groups of three or four children working together are particularly effective. In such groups the children will take turns being the moderator, the recorder/reporter, or the monitor of the group's progress.

BALANCE

Teachers in the early grades, especially those who lean toward developmentally appropriate teaching, talk a good deal about the need for balance. Balance means quiet times followed by active times followed by quiet times; times when children work alone and times when they work with others; times for physical activity and times for activities directed toward social and emotional development; times to explore and times to consolidate learning. The days must be varied and should address the needs of the "whole child."

ASSESSMENT

Assessment refers to determinations about children's progress. More and more educational professionals, at least those involved in early childhood education, recommend that we stop relying on traditional standardized tests, which evaluate children on the basis of fixed standards of skill, achievement, or intelligence. Children's growth is uneven throughout the primary years. In these early years, children are acquiring the skills they will need for continued success in school, and these skills are in a fluid, ever-changing state. Teachers should not make judgments that contribute to failure by attaching negative labels or by separating children into "good," "average," or "slow learner" groups. Standardized tests, however, often imply and contribute to such labels or separations.

The current trend in the lower grades of elementary school is away from standardized testing. I do not recommend the use of standardized tests before grade 4, and even in the upper elementary grades their benefits are uncertain. Instead of using tests, teachers can assess students by keeping ongoing records of performance, documenting students' work on a day-by-day basis. Teachers also keep portfolios of children's work; these are available for parents to review. At the third grade level, teachers also guide children in systematic and regular self-evaluation. By asking, for example, "Do you feel that you understood what we talked about in science today? Do you think you could explain it to a friend? What do you think was most difficult?" teachers encourage children to define their own learning processes and help set goals.

THE TEACHER AS FACILITATOR

A facilitator is someone who makes it easier for another to do something. Teachers who guide, question, and support children in their learning are facilitators; they make it easier for children to learn, but they give the central role in the learning process to the children themselves. Teachers who see themselves as facilitators stimulate children and challenge them to think and question. They provide a diversity of materials and activities, and they search for new books and questions that will extend children's learning and enlarge their awareness. They spend much of their time supporting children's investigations. In contrast, teachers who "give answers" most of the time and who do most of the talking in the classroom are not facilitators.

3 *Your Child's School Day*

What is your child's school day like? Although each teacher will organize his or her class somewhat differently, what follows is a fairly typical day in a third grade classroom that is organized around the principles of developmental learning.

8:30–9:00 A.M.

The classroom is open when the first child arrives in the morning. The teacher greets the children as they come in and helps them get involved in interesting activities. They may, for example, sit quietly with another child and visit, begin reading, start writing a story, or try out one of the new computer programs. Essentially, this is a time for everyone to get comfortable with the beginning of another school day.

9:00–9:30 A.M.

The children gather for the formal opening activity. The teacher usually begins with the news of the day: birthdays, visitors, new materials, or special events. This is followed by announcements the children wish to make, perhaps about something interesting they have observed, a new word or song they have learned, or a funny or scary experience. The teacher then records what everyone is planning to do during the day and what groups she will call together for particular activities.

9:30–10:00 A.M.

Everyone (including the teacher) selects a book and reads quietly.

10:00–11:30 A.M.

Children carry out their plans for the morning. The teacher guides and challenges the children in her role as a facilitator of learning. During this time the teacher also has individual conferences with students.

11:30 A.M.–Noon

The children gather for a story. In many schools teachers stop reading aloud to children after grade 2. I recommend that they continue reading regularly to their classes through grade 6. Older children benefit by being read to because many children, even skilled readers, have greater oral than written comprehension—that is, they have better understanding of what they hear than of what they read, so they can be introduced to more complex, colorful, and sophisticated materials through oral reading. Read-aloud sessions also provide children with some quiet time during which their energies are focused on listening and thinking. The teacher may encourage the children to think about and discuss the story by asking questions: "If there were five children in the family instead of one, how would it have been different?" "How could we change the ending of the story?" "What other characters would we need if we changed the ending of the story?" Of course, not all of the stories will lend themselves to these or similar questions; sometimes it is better to let the story stand on its own, without comments or questions.

Noon–12:40 P.M.
Break time for lunch and outdoor play.

12:40–1:00 P.M.
Gathering time and planning time. The teacher guides the children through such questions as "What do I have left to finish before I go home?" "What questions do I have?" "Have I completed work in the math area, the science area?" "Have I read a book?" "What project am I working on?" "How long will I need to finish my project?"

1:00–2:10 P.M.
Large block of time to work. The teacher circulates, questions, gathers small groups of children together to work on various skills as needed, and gives support and encouragement to the children as they proceed with their activities.

2:10–2:25 P.M.
Break time, often outside play time.

2:25–3:00 P.M.
Sustained Silent Writing (SSW) and Writer's Workshops. Children put their ideas onto paper. The teacher will often bring small groups of children together for a writing lesson, perhaps focusing on ways of using quotation marks and exclamation marks, or introducing alternative vocabulary words. Every child finds a way to express

himself or herself in writing, especially during this period but also at other times of the school day.

3:00–3:30 P.M.

The children show or share some of the things they have been working on. They add finished work to their folders. They put things that they are still working on into their working files, all ready for the next day. During this time they reflect on the day's activities. The teacher may encourage them to ask themselves, Which of the activities was most interesting? What will I work on tomorrow? What am I going to tell my parents about tonight? What book will I read at home? At this point the teacher might also outline a homework assignment.

3:30–3:40 P.M.

Gradual dismissal, with good-byes to everyone.

What Your Child Learns in School

This chapter is an overview of the typical curriculum for the third grade and is intended to give you an idea of what your child is learning. But because children learn in different ways and at different rates, not all children will grasp a particular part of the curriculum at the same time. While most third grade children will master what is outlined below as the common third grade curriculum, others will need more time to solidify their understanding of some subjects. Teachers and parents who understand development, who do not view the curriculum in terms of rigid grades or steps, will accept this as quite normal.

I have outlined third grade content, but keep in mind that some elements from the previous year's curriculum are carried into the third grade; there is typically a good deal of overlap in the primary grades. And while I have divided the curriculum into different subject areas for convenience, in reality the boundaries between subject areas are not always clearly drawn in these early years. Parents should also be aware that teaching in the first few grades is more informal than formal. Much of what children learn comes through activities and concrete experiences rather than through a teacher imparting information.

One last point needs to be made about the curriculum. I have refrained from listing all of the *specific* elements that make up the various curriculum areas: the math facts that are learned, the books that are read, the historical figures who are presented. Teachers must introduce children at every grade level to a diverse and rich array of literature and to the many people who make up the traditions of their communities and of the country; at the same time, they must involve children in the fullest use of mathematics, science, and the like. The curriculum should always be expansive, never limiting. A good curriculum is flexible, so that the teacher can easily add not only new subject matter but new levels of complexity. The teacher's main responsibility throughout elementary school is to ensure that children maintain a sense of curiosity, that they love reading and writing, and that they take an ongoing interest in the world around them. The teacher's job is to help children become and remain active and confident learners.

In doing this job, teachers will probably use a good deal of traditional children's literature. But they may find that songs or stories from their children's cultural heritages have greater potential to stimulate children's language development and expand their learning. Similarly, the traditional heroes and narratives of United States history will surely emerge in the classroom. But knowing that the traditional histories often excluded women and persons of color, teachers will take care to expose the children to other, less traditional heroes and narratives. And by using math in many different ways, children not only learn number facts of the 6x6=36 variety but also absorb the rules governing addition, subtraction, multiplication, and division. They will also come to see and understand the patterns and relationships by which numbers are governed.

The curriculum throughout the primary grades should be rich and full of diverse starting points so that each child—with his or her individual interests, learning styles, and level of development—can enter fully into the learning process. And the curriculum must always be intellectually challenging.

As I noted in the introduction, teachers should be expected to have clear goals for the children they teach. They should be able to explain what the children will understand, or be able to do, by the end of the school year, and how everything they do in the classroom is related to those goals. Teachers should also be able to explain how they assess each child's progress toward those goals and how they will stay in touch with parents.

The Third Grade Curriculum

Most children entering the third grade can read and write. They will, however, need continuing support in their use of language. Classrooms must maintain a developmental atmosphere geared to each child's level of skill and growth. The curriculum should evolve upward, growing mostly out of what the children have learned in the earlier grades. I say this because there has been a tendency in the schools to push curriculum downward—so that, for example, material that was once part of the fourth grade curriculum becomes the subject matter of the third grade. This trend has been detrimental, because it has resulted in an increasingly *information-oriented* curriculum in the lower grades, when an *activity-oriented* curriculum better serves the needs of the developing learner.

By the third grade, most children are able to read independently. This means that they are able to read a wide range of books, allowing the teacher to present them with an ever-growing diversity of reading and learning experiences. Moreover, third grade children are generally able to read for information as well as enjoyment.

The third grade is typically seen as the completion of the primary years of school—the basic years that are the foundation for later learning. (The upper grades of elementary school—grades 4, 5, and 6—are sometimes thought of as intermediate years.) By *the end* of the third grade children are expected to be reasonably confident readers and writers; to understand the patterns of mathematical relationships and to be able to use math to solve basic computational problems; to know how to approach science questions; to be careful observers of the natural environment; to understand the importance of good health; to understand historical time, seeing history as a human story; to appreciate the interdependency of people in their communities and across the nation and the world; to see themselves and their families as producers and consumers; to comprehend geographical relationships such as direction and geographical concepts such as place, elevation, latitude, and longitude; to enjoy the arts and recognize their place in society; and to see themselves as creators in various art forms. Above all, it is hoped that third grade children will be curious about the world, understand that they can learn and be filled with the desire to do so, and be optimistic.

READING

In the area of reading, the teacher's principal goal is that the children view reading as central to learning and as a source of endless information and enjoyment. The teacher also wants each child to gain confidence about being a successful reader. More specifically, the third grade curriculum is designed to ensure that children become more skilled in identifying and using the title, table of contents, glossary, and index of a book; understand more fully the roles of the authors and illustrators of the books they read; readily identify the setting, main characters, and plot of a story; use the dictionary, thesaurus, encyclopedia, almanac, and newspaper, as well as maps; read a variety of books in all curriculum areas; and expand their range of reading in children's magazines and newspapers. The teacher also wants the children to continue their personal libraries at home; to increase the time spent in silent reading; to dramatize what they read; to express their ideas fully, understanding that there are different viewpoints; to see connections between what they read and their own lives; to understand the multiple meanings of words; and to increase their familiarity with the library. Teachers should, as I noted earlier, continue to read to children daily, using a broad array of children's literature that includes stories from different cultures.

WRITING

Writing is closely related to reading. Teachers make sure that children write every day and see themselves as authors. Children are encouraged to keep journals and to write to one another, to their parents and grandparents, and to classroom visitors; pen-pal correspondences with children in other communities or countries are common. The children also write books. The teacher continues to support invented or transitional spelling, but children are encouraged to pay more attention to punctuation and its relationship to meaning; to the fact that many words have several different meanings, and that some words work better than others in certain contexts; to the sequence of events and ideas in stories; to the personal nature of writing; and to the possibilities of revision. In regard to revision, the children participate actively in writing workshops where they share their writing and begin outlines of new writing. They also keep portfolios of their writings—works in progress as well as completed works. Their portfolios help them see that their writing over time offers material for self-evaluation. Third grade writers use prefixes and suffixes, compound words, different tenses, and synonyms and antonyms to add variety to their writing. It is in the third grade that children shift from printing to cursive writing, with an understanding that legibility is important; by the end of grade 3, most children should be writing in cursive most of the time.

LISTENING AND SPEAKING

The oral aspects of language are important and are closely related to the development of children's reading, writing, and thinking skills. Teachers allow children to gain considerable experience in telling and retelling stories, speaking informally, sharing information with classmates and visitors, leaving and taking telephone messages, and distinguishing fact from make-believe. Focused discussion activities are also important; here the teacher guides the children in a slightly more formal discussion of a selected topic. In addition, children participate in readers' theater and plays. They read poetry aloud, learning to match their volume and inflection to the demands of the subject matter. The teacher helps them explore the differences in intensity of various words and speech patterns.

MATHEMATICS

Mathematics in grade 3 builds on what the child has already learned; experience in using math is a process of continuous growth. Although third graders are introduced to new, more complex forms of math, the study of mathematics remains more concrete than abstract—most numbers stand for something that the children can see. Children are helped to understand that mathematics is something logical, not merely a random collection of facts, and that numbers are linked together by relationships that can be grasped. Third graders use math in the course of working with science, cooking, health, social studies, reading, and writing. They are able to read numbers into the thousands, both as numerals and as words. The idea of zero will become clearer, and children will use it in their computations. Third graders learn the position of 100s and 1,000s; they gain greater understanding of fractions such as $\frac{1}{4}$, $\frac{1}{8}$, $\frac{1}{3}$, $\frac{2}{3}$, and $\frac{1}{10}$ and their relationship to wholes; they estimate more confidently; they conduct precise measurements in inches, feet, yards, ounces, and pounds; and they use graphs to represent numerical comparisons. They add columns of three or four numbers with regrouping, subtract numbers in the thousands, have good recall of addition and subtraction through the number 20, begin using division, learn liquid capacities and measurements, and begin using Fahrenheit and Celsius scales on a thermometer. Children become increasingly aware of the *patterns* of mathematics, including the relationships among addition, subtraction, and multiplication. They also do more computations in the form of word or story problems.

SCIENCE

The natural world is the basis of most science study in the third grade, just as it was in the earlier years. The teacher's primary goal is to foster the children's sense of curiosity about the world and their skills of inquiry. Teachers will make frequent use of questions that stimulate the critical thinking of the children: Why is that? How does that happen? What if . . . ?

Science study should be very active in the early primary years. Whenever possible, children interact directly with science materials and observe phenomena firsthand. They learn about pollution and the problems it causes; they become familiar with the relationships between oceans, seas, rivers, and ponds; they study animals and plants in increasing detail; they learn about the different planets and the solar system; they use simple machines; they experiment with electricity, principally through batteries and bulbs; they begin to understand the history of life on earth; and they add scientific terms—matter, environment, machine, heat, electricity, extinction, and experiment—to their vocabularies. They will observe the moon and stars, learn more about the sun, use telescopes, build and stock terraria, and study rocks and other geological formations.

HEALTH

In the primary grades, health is closely allied to science and social studies. Learning to care for and respect one's body is an important part of the curriculum. Children continue to learn about the relationship between nutrition and health, and they gain greater understanding of calories, grams, cholesterol, fats, proteins, and carbohydrates. Third graders also study the effects of food additives, the role of advertising in food choices, and the relationship between fast foods and nutrition. They learn more about wellness, disease and its prevention, the importance of cleanliness, the dangers of smoking and of drugs, and the role of exercise in physical development. They study the parts of the body—bones, muscles, organs, and the circulatory system. (Children are especially fascinated by the brain.) As in the earlier grades, safety is stressed. Children learn basic safety rules for the playground, the street, the bicycle, and the home; they also learn simple first aid. Topics such as making and keeping friends, getting home safely, and what it means to be a "couch potato" are the subjects of class discussion. Third grade children also continue learning about human sexuality; as in earlier grades, this basically means that their questions are answered frankly but simply.

SOCIAL STUDIES

A large part of the social studies curriculum throughout the primary grades consists of learning about families, neighborhoods, cities and towns, and countries. Third graders focus their attention on their own communities and states—on landmarks, architecture, history, changes over time, commerce, distinctive features, and similarities to other communities. They explore the differences between urban, suburban, and rural communities. They also learn about and celebrate various local, state, and national holidays and festivals. They read biographies of important Americans. The concept of citizenship is emphasized, usually in ways that promote responsibility, such as helping others and learning about rules and how rules are used to resolve conflicts. Children will be asked to talk with their parents about voting and governmental functions. And they will be encouraged to do some community service. They will also interview their parents and grandparents about their cultural heritage. Teachers will use every opportunity to help children understand other cultures in different parts of the world. A child's view of the world expands in the third grade. Maps will become more familiar, and children will be able to use map coordinates, read map symbols, and locate oceans, rivers, cities, and towns. One key aspect of third grade social studies is that children will show increased understanding of historical time. They will also learn to be historians, doing their own research (interviewing family members and others and reading books, newspapers, and magazines) and writing their own personal, family, or community histories in the form of time lines or stories.

THE ARTS

Children should be encouraged to participate in all forms of artistic expression throughout the elementary grades. Self-expression through singing, painting, dancing, and acting can do wonders for a child's confidence and self-esteem while strengthening his or her communication skills; and exposure to a variety of artists and performers in many media provides the foundation for lifelong enjoyment of the arts. Unfortunately, however, arts programs are being dropped from many schools, sacrificed either because of budget problems or because policy makers have decided that the arts are not as important as other elements of the curriculum. Parents must insist on strong arts programs for their children.

Children are particularly drawn to painting as a means of self-expression. They should also have opportunities to make music and to dance. The third grade is a time for children to be actively engaged *in* the arts rather than simply learning *about* the arts. But their imaginations can be stimulated and challenged by visits to museums and exhibitions or by musical and dance performances. This is a good time for children to begin lessons on musical instruments; schools should provide these lessons to ensure full access by *all* children.

5 Conversations with Your Child

This chapter presents an array of "conversation starters" for you to use with your third grade child. I use the term *conversation* broadly, to include both question-and-answer dialogues and a variety of games and activities. The conversation starters are grouped by subject matter: the language arts and the creative arts, math, science and health, and social studies. Most of the ideas and suggestions I offer are broad and open-ended; some, however, are quite specific. And many of the conversation starters can be adapted and expanded by imaginative parents (and children) for an almost infinite number of possibilities.

Some of the conversations that are introduced in this volume of the *101 Educational Conversations You Should Have with Your Child* series appeared in the earlier volume, *101 Educational Conversations with Your Second Grader*. Most of these, however, have been reframed to accommodate the greater maturity and knowledge of the third grader. Such overlapping will also occur in later volumes of the series. In part this overlapping occurs because the curriculum is often interconnected from year to year. But the overlap also reflects the developmental character of learning—the same ideas are right for different children at different ages. And returning to the same conversations or activities a year or more from now will let you see how your child's knowledge and understanding have grown.

The conversation starters are a way for you to discover what your child knows and understands in relation to what is typically taught in the schools. You should remember, however, that the curriculum is not identical in every school; a gap in your child's learning may simply mean that that particular subject has not yet been introduced in the classroom. Be satisfied if your child can engage in *most* of these conversations, even with partial knowledge or limited understanding. You can always return to problem areas later on, as your child's mastery increases. But what about areas of learning that appear to be entirely outside a child's knowledge? A third grade child, for example, may appear to know very little about how to read a map. While map reading is part of the curriculum in most schools, I do not believe that this gap in knowledge is necessarily a serious problem; parents themselves can help children with this kind of learning. But the parents might, nonetheless, ask the child's teacher, "What are you doing to help the children work with maps?" On the other hand, if a third grade child shows little interest in writing, the parents should certainly talk with the teacher, even as they spend more time writing with their child at home.

These ideas have been framed as conversational exchanges or playful interactions, not as daily quizzes. They are designed to promote interaction between parents and children. And because conversation does not flourish when questions lend themselves to simple answers—"yes," "no," and "I don't know"—most of the questions and activities have an open-ended quality. Try not to make them seem like tests, or like some form of Trivial Pursuit. Instead, work them naturally into the time you spend with your child. The conversations should occur in a relaxed, comfortable context—at dinner, during a walk or a game, perhaps in relation to shared television programs or movies, or at some quiet time.

In a fundamental way, these conversations are educational opportunities. They allow you not only to reinforce what your child's teacher is doing but to expand the teacher's efforts, enriching your child's education. I believe that parents will, in the process of engaging in the conversations, realize more fully that they too are important and capable teachers. An additional benefit is that parents who take part in these exchanges will show their children that learning is a valuable activity, one that is capable of providing pleasure and worthy of respect.

The conversations are built around some important assumptions. I have assumed that parents

- Read to their children frequently.

- Listen to their children, respond to their questions, and engage them in ongoing conversations.

- Find opportunities to play with their children—physically active games as well as board games.

- Take walks with their children—around the block, through the parks, to a local playground.

- Take their children to the library, zoos, museums, and nature trails.

- Listen to records and tapes with their children.

- Let their children help them cook, wash the car, or rake leaves.

■ Watch television with their children and discuss the content of programs with them.

■ Share family stories with their children.

By enjoying their children regularly and naturally in the course of these and other activities, parents come to know a great deal about their children's growth as learners. The questions, activities, and ideas in this chapter will tell parents even more about their children—particularly about what their children are learning in school.

As you go through these conversations, keep in mind that third grade children are in the process of consolidating many ideas and relationships. Rather than recognizing words in isolation or memorizing a lot of facts, children are striving for deeper understanding and for mastery of skills. If, for example, children learn various number facts but cannot use them for purposes they actually understand, math is not becoming a particularly important subject matter.

All-Purpose Conversation Starters

Many conversations between you and your child can arise spontaneously from day-to-day events. You can create numerous opportunities for such interactions in the following ways:

■ Look at all the materials your child brings home from school. You will see a variety of things, including work sheets, word lists, books, classification exercises, writing samples, sculptures, paintings, and sketches. Ask your child about them. Say, "This looks interesting. Can you tell me how you did it?" or "I see you are learning to set up science experiments. What problems are you studying? What have you learned?" Remember to be supportive rather than judgmental. If your child does not regularly bring writing, books, drawings, constructions, experiments, or paintings home from school, you should be concerned.

■ Observe your child at play. You will see that your child often acts out or imitates school activities, stories, things seen on television, and the actions and speech patterns of family members. Such acting out is an important part of the learning process. It also gives parents many starting points for conversations, through remarks such as "You really do like writing letters" or "You seem to be enjoying soccer a lot."

By looking closely at what your child brings home from school and how your child acts out new knowledge or skills while playing, you can keep in touch with your child's education. These observations form a significant part of what you know about your child.

Certain questions that promote conversation between you and your child are versatile enough to apply in just about any situation. They may already be part of your repertoire. If not, start working them into your conversations. Use them often, but always—to repeat a point I made earlier in this chapter—use them patiently and naturally.

The questions are: "I wonder why that is?" "What do you think is happening?" "Is there any other way to do it?" "What if you tried it that way?" These questions and the many variations you can invent not only help keep dialogue going but also stimulate inquiry and discovery.

Language and the Arts

During the early years, children need to acquire confidence in their ability to read and write. The biggest key to effective reading and writing is exposure to a broad range of language and its uses; this is how children gain understanding of what language can do. The schools will contribute to this understanding through the stories teachers read, the records and tapes children listen to, and the many intentional elaborations of words and word meanings teachers provide. But the home is also important in these early years. Try to read a broad range of literature to your child: rhymes, poems, fables, folktales, classic stories, and biographies. Sing songs together and play games. Such experiences will make a critical difference in your child's development. In addition, call attention to things in newspapers and magazines, leave written messages around for your child, and make sure that your *own* literacy is evident. It is important for your child to see you reading and writing—and enjoying it.

You should try to do some reading with your child on a regular basis. As a third grader's schedule will usually be more active than that of younger children, you may find that it is not as easy as it once was to schedule daily reading together. At a minimum, try to spend some time on Sunday afternoons or evenings to read from authors such as Charles Dickens, Robert Louis Stevenson, James Fenimore Cooper, Charlotte Brontë, Jack London, Bret Harte, or Louisa May Alcott. Your child's interest in the stories you read will tell you a great deal about his or her developing listening and comprehension skills.

Using the basic format of one of the stories you read, write a story together with your child. You write the first few lines or paragraph, have your child write the second few lines or paragraph, and so on.

This could be a long-term project that gives you a look at your child's understanding of story sequence and word meanings; it also encourages the child to write creatively.

Read newspaper headlines together and try to figure out what the story is about. This will help make the newspaper important to your child, as well as provide reading practice.

Keep adding new words to your conversations. This is one means of expanding your child's language base.

It is important that children know the names of objects in their environment; this is a base for future learning. You can gain insight into what your child knows by playing games. You might look at a photograph or illustration and say, "Let's find all the pine trees, birch trees, water towers, skyscrapers, grain elevators, movie theaters," and so on.

Give each other words, with the idea that you are to make up a story around the word. This is an interesting way to see what words your child is learning and how he or she understands them.

Committing things to memory is a good exercise for the early years. Each of you memorize a poem or story to tell to the other.

Play games based on words. For example, say, "I can visualize something that is blue and white and round and is in the living room. What is it?" You and your child take turns. Keep adding variables—size, substance, or use—to the descriptions.

As you read a story to your child, occasionally ask, "What does that remind you of? What do you see in your mind?" Mental images are important to ongoing learning. You and your child might even try sketching the images.

Folktales and myths are typically part of the third grade curriculum. See what your child knows about Robin Hood, Johnny Appleseed, Paul Bunyan, King Arthur, Brer Rabbit, Zeus, Apollo, or Prometheus. Read folktales and myths to each other.

Read signs together as you go for walks: stop signs, street names, product signs, billboards, and the names on cars, trucks, and buildings.

Say, "Let's see how many words we can think of that begin with *E,* with *G,* with *W.*" You can also use "words that have the *oo* sound in them," "words that end in *T,*" or anything else you think of. This game reinforces some of the language work being done in school. It lets you see how well your child is hearing the various sounds—the components of words—and also shows the growth in your child's vocabulary.

Shopping provides many opportunities to learn language and math. For example, you might say, "Can you get me six cans of tomato soup?" or four cans of pork and beans, or two boxes of cereal (name some particular cereals). You might ask for several different types of products at once; the number of items and categories should increase over time. Also see how many labels your child can read as you go through the store.

Teach your child something that was important to you as a child—a folktale, a particular nursery rhyme related to your cultural background, a song. Or remind your child of a story or rhyme that he or she liked a few years earlier. See how much your child retains and understands over time.

Say, "Let's think of all the things we know that are noisy, quiet, nearby, far away, green, mushy, slippery, very heavy, light as a feather, fast as light, slow as molasses."

Play a word association game. You start by saying a word; your child is to say the first thing he or she thinks of. Then your child gives you a word, and so on.

Listen to music together. Talk about how it makes you feel—like "just sitting," "dreaming," "dancing," "marching." Move together to music. Also, share your views. This will help your child enjoy music and also let you watch your child's music awareness grow.

As another language-expanding conversation that will also tell you how much your child knows about many aspects of the world, say, "Let's tell each other all we know about the Mississippi River." (Or maple trees, hawks, hurricanes, whales, the Iroquois Indians, the moon, particular cities, outer space, electricity, engines, airplanes, and so on.) You can see what words your child knows as well as introduce new words, concepts, and ideas. This kind of activity is almost limitless. But you must listen carefully to your child's expressions. Do not be too hasty to correct or interrupt with information you think your child should know; that can come later, at the end of the game or in a different conversation. It is important to let children express themselves fully instead of immediately quenching their pleasure with corrections.

Give your child a simple model of an airplane, a boat, a house, furniture, or a car to put together, following the instructions that are given. How effectively does he or she follow the directions? Does he or she seem to grasp what to do? From time to time experiment with a more complex model, perhaps even one you draw and build together.

Authorship is an important part of reading and writing. Ask your child about his or her favorite authors. Talk about new books together. Check out new titles in the library. See how many books by your child's favorite authors are in the library.

Use birthdays, holidays, or special family times as occasions for writing. Ask your child to write a letter to a grandmother, grandfather, or other close relative. Writing can be encouraged in lots of ways. For example, leave notes for your child, and ask him or her to leave notes for you. When you read what your child has written, pay more attention to the ideas, the inventions, and the sustained stories than to spelling and punctuation—although you will notice that your child's spelling and sentence structure will become more conventional over time, as he or she gains mastery of these writing skills. Encourage your child to write stories and poems. A third grade child might also enjoy keeping a journal, diary, or memory book.

On a fairly regular basis, ask your child to bring home a favorite book from school to read to you. After your child has read the book, ask what he or she likes most about the story. As you listen to your child read the book, you will gain a good sense of your child's growth as a reader. Do not be alarmed if he or she skips a word occasionally, or reads "home" as "house." Is the story coherent and understandable as your child reads it? Is your child's reading fluent or is it halting, with long stops between words?

Look at paintings together, either at museums or in books and magazines. Van Gogh, Gauguin, and Picasso have a great deal of appeal to children; you might also give some attention to abstract and geometric art. Ask your child what he or she likes in each painting. You will gain some insight into your child's growing understanding of color and into his or her imagination.

Ask often how your child likes various artworks—paintings, architecture, photographs, and music. This is your way of saying that you value artistic expression and of keeping your child's interest high.

Say, "Let's think of all the things rain does." It falls, splashes, drops, makes puddles, and so on. Continue the exercise with wind, a tornado, the sun, the moon, an animal, or any other noun that might suggest a variety of action words to your child.

Ask your child to look up the meaning of a word in the dictionary, a state in the atlas, or a person or city in the encyclopedia. You will see how familiar your child is with the use of these resources.

Begin to play games around antonyms (opposite words), such as hot-cold, light-dark, black-white, hard-soft; or synonyms (words with similar but slightly different meanings), such as evening-night, red-crimson, polite-courteous; or homonyms (words that are pronounced the same but have different meanings), such as sail-sale, tail-tale, two-too. For example, you could say, "I'll say a word and then you say the opposite." Or "Let's list all the words that sound the same."

Stay in touch with your child's reading. What is he or she learning about biography and autobiography, fiction and nonfiction, prose and poetry? Does he or she know what those terms mean?

Suggest that your child write a letter to a public individual or organization about a cause that concerns him or her—to the National Wildlife Federation, for example, about endangered or threatened species in your state, or to the mayor of your city about a local issue. The conventions of this type of letter should have been part of your child's third grade curriculum.

Early in their school careers children should be encouraged to assess their own progress as learners. In relation to reading and the language arts, ask your child such questions as, "How is your writing coming along?" "What causes you difficulty?" "What do you most enjoy writing?" Your child's responses to these questions will probably give you hints about games, activities, or pastimes to share with your child to boost his or her learning; they will also serve as a starting point for your own conversations with your child's teacher.

Mathematics

Like language, math is a subject in which it is important for children to build confidence. Third grade children continue to study quantities, size, scale, and estimation. Discussions of these qualities include increased attention to mastering addition, subtraction, division, and multiplication. The more concrete the learning, and the more children are encouraged to see mathematics in use all around them, the better. You can help by using math and the language of math around the house. When measuring, have your child hold one end of the tape; talk about splitting apples into halves and quarters; describe activities in terms of order and sequence, using words like "first," "second," "twelfth," and "thirteenth"; keep a growth chart of your child; use numbers aloud when you are counting things; make estimates and judgments about distance and time; play a lot of number-oriented games. Math is a natural area of learning that should always be interesting to children.

Count to 24 by fours, to 30 by sixes, to 40 by eights.

Make up story problems around math facts such as 12-4=8. For example, 12 elephants started the race but 4 stopped along the way; how many finished? If the stories are silly or funny, so much the better.

Another way to see how well your child understands numbers is to play board games that call for markers to be moved forward and backward so many spaces—for example, "Now you can move six spaces forward." A considerable amount of mathematics is embedded in games such as dominoes and Monopoly. Chess, which involves strategy as well as mathematics, would be a particularly good game to introduce and play.

Many games will reveal your child's knowledge of numbers as well as of words and directions. Play tic-tac-toe, dots, checkers, concentration, hangman, Scrabble, and increasingly complex card games.

Ask your child to use a ruler to measure something in the house—a rectangular table, a room, a bookshelf. You will learn a good deal about your child's measurement skills.

See how many math symbols or notations you and your child can find in the newspaper. Such symbols might include +, -, =, ½, 10:15, a date such as 6/30/92, shapes such as a circle or triangle, or graphs.

There are many opportunities for counting during everyday activities. While cooking you could ask, "Can you count out eight potatoes?" or ask, "Can you put ten cookies and four apples on the plate for dessert?"

While cooking or baking, ask your child to read the recipe and measure the quantities of ingredients called for: three and a half tablespoons of sugar, two and a quarter cups of flour, and the like. This is a good way to see your child put math to use.

Fractions are part of the math curriculum in the third grade. Ask your child to explain, with examples, such fractions as $\frac{1}{8}$, $\frac{1}{16}$, and $\frac{1}{32}$. Find such measurements on a ruler, a graph, a measuring cup, or a jar.

With a stopwatch, see how quickly your child can run 40 yards. Together, record and graph the times over several weeks. There is an almost limitless number of activities of this kind. You can also move into calculations such as, "How fast did you go per second in feet? In yards?" Or "If you continued to run at the same speed, how long would it take you to run 400 yards? How about 600 yards?"

Use numbers to refer your child to articles or pictures in magazines or newspapers. Say, "There is an interesting story about a horse on page 4, section B."

Make up problems. For example: "It takes us 30 minutes to get to Uncle Jack's house. He wants us there by 6:00. When should we leave?" Or "If we travel 30 miles an hour, how long will it take us to get to a town 10 miles away?"

Computations of weight, size, and scale are important. You might pose such questions as "Which of these two objects is heavier?" (Or lighter, longer, shorter, thicker, thinner.) Also you could ask, "How can we be sure?" This leads your child to use his or her measuring and estimating skills.

Your third grade child is using three- and four-digit numbers. Does he or she understand that 24 is two 10s and four 1s? That 124 is twelve 10s and four 1s? That 1,240 is 124 tens (or 12 hundreds and four 10s)? Ask your child to explain these numbers.

Your child will regularly be using a calculator in grade 3. Ask him or her to help you with computational problems such as your checkbook, budget, floor covering measurements, and the like.

Your child should be able to add and subtract double- and triple-digit numbers. Take turns making up problems for each other. For example: 26+12, 26-14, 54+12, 54-12, 154+124, 154-124.

Third graders will typically learn the multiplication tables up through 10. Over the course of the year you and your child can work through such multiplication activities as 3x2=6, 3x3=9, 6x3=18, 6x4=24, and so on. Can your child devise a story problem to go with a multiplication exercise? (For example, 6x6 might translate into "Six kids watched six videotapes each. How many videotapes did they watch all together?")

Work on a "map" of mathematical concepts. For example, *shape* might be your starting point. Write SHAPE in the center of a large piece of paper, and then draw all the images connected with shape: triangles (all kinds), circles, cubes, squares, hexagons, and cylinders, as well as examples of shapes in use, such as architecture, art forms, animals, trees, and so on. Use connecting lines to link connected shapes—all the triangular objects might be linked with red lines, for example, and the rectangular objects with blue lines.

Estimate together the amount of wastepaper products, cans, or glass containers your family uses each week. Then ask your child to figure how how much there would be each month and each year and how much, on average, for each person in the household each week, month, and year. This exercise lets your child not only use his or her estimating, multiplying, and dividing skills but also encourages close examination of consumer habits.

Children must understand the relationships between numbers, not merely the rote tables of addition and multiplication. Does your child realize, for example, that 20x12 can be reached by doubling numbers: that 20x2=40, 20x4=80, 20x6=120, and so on? That 9x6 is the same as 9x3x2? And furthermore that 9x6 is 9x5+9? That 2x5 is 2+2+2+2+2?

Ask your child, "How well do you understand the math you are studying in school? What are you having difficulty with? Do you think you need help? What kind of help would be best?" Again, your child's responses may guide your interactions with both the child and his or her teacher.

Science and Health

Science study in the third grade remains concerned with the natural world—wind and rain, ponds, rivers, lakes, streams, the solar system, animals and plants, and food chains. Children observe nature and learn how things move through their various life cycles. The primary grades are a time to keep curiosity alive and to provide children with good skills in observation and problem solving.

Close observation is a primary objective of the science program. You and your child can examine a rock, a tree, a leaf, an animal, or an insect. Take turns asking, "What do you see?"

Observe the sky together. Ask, "What shapes do you see in the clouds?" "Where will you find the sun in the early morning?" "At noon?" "In the evening?"

Observe the moon together over several weeks; note whether you are looking at it at the same time every day or at different times. Note its location and draw its various shapes; be aware of the stars around it. Examine the moon chart in the weather section of your daily newspaper or on a calendar.

Can your child locate the North Star? Can he or she explain how it has helped explorers and outdoorspeople?

Ask about the scientists your child has studied. What does he or she know about them?

Walks afford many opportunities to identify objects in the environment. You can ask, "What do you think that is?" "What kind of bird is that?" "Let's see how many different kinds of flowers we can identify in this block" (or park, or outdoor mall).

Together you and your child can name various parts of the body: the heart, lungs, blood, and bones. Talk about their functions.

Ask why it is important to get exercise, to rest, to eat well, to dress appropriately for various weather conditions, and to see a doctor when you are sick. See what your child is learning about health.

Engage in physical exercise together. Point out how important exercise is to good health. This is a good invitation to ask your child what he or she is learning about staying healthy.

Science in school increasingly gives attention to the sources of common things and to everyday processes. You and your child can investigate questions such as "Where does our water come from?" "Where does our sewage go?" "What is the source of our electricity?" "How does a motor work?" "How does a plant grow?" "What causes the cement to crack?"

Make a game of identifying sounds you and your child hear: trees rustling, water running, pots and pans banging, dogs barking, helicopters whirring, lawn mowers chugging.

Do simple science experiments with your child. For example, ask, "If I wanted to know whether the jar full of sand was heavier or lighter than the jar full of rocks, what would I do?" Or "How could we determine which kind of paper towel would hold the most water?" Such experiments give a good indication of your child's thinking processes.

Examine a single tree (if you and your child have done this exercise before, be sure to pick a different kind of tree this time). See what your child notices: the shape, the size, the texture of the bark, the colors of the leaves. You can make seasonal observations of the leaves at different stages or of the tree's fruits or seeds. Sketch the tree at different times of the year.

Watch nature programs on television with your child. They offer opportunities for interesting conversations about new things your child has learned. Your child's level of interest, and the questions he or she asks are good indications of what the child is learning in school about nature.

Ask about parts of the food chain—for instance, "What does a fish eat? What might eat a fish?"

Children tend to be greatly interested in water. You could ask your child which of several objects—a rotted piece of wood, a solid piece of wood, a marble, an empty aluminum can, a full aluminum can, a metal screw, a plastic cup—will float and which will sink. Ask why some float and others sink. You will see how far your child has developed the ability to formulate possible reasons for what happens.

Ask your child to draw the solar system with as many planets as he or she can. This exercise will let you see what your child understands about the solar system. Try it at different times to see how the child's knowledge is growing.

Have your child check the thermometer each morning and evening. Make some graphs together—for example, you could show the differences between morning and evening temperatures over a week. Compare the temperatures with those recorded the year before, or five years before, or with average and record high and low temperatures. Daily weather broadcasts give the average and record temperatures for each day; you and your child could consult old newspapers at the library for previous years' temperatures.

The life cycle is a large element of primary school science; this is one of the reasons students keep mice and hamsters, hatch chicken eggs, and watch caterpillars turn into butterflies. It is also why many primary classrooms have made ties to senior centers and have invited mothers to bring their infants to class on occasion. See what your child has observed about baby mice, hamsters, chickens, or butterflies—or about human infants or older people. If he or she has questions, suggest ways of finding out the answers.

In regard to nutrition, ask your child if he or she knows which foods are high in fat, protein, carbohydrates, cholesterol, and caffeine. Make a practice of reading nutrition labels together when you are shopping for or preparing food.

Study nature together. In a natural setting, through books, or both, examine the habitats of various animals, noting the similarities and differences between different habitats. What can your child tell you about the animals you see and how they live?

See what your child knows about microscopes and telescopes. Ask whether he or she is using such instruments in school. Children like to demonstrate new skills and knowledge—ask your child to show you how a microscope or telescope works.

Visit a planetarium with your child. Before you go, discuss the program to see what your child already knows. After the show, talk about what each of you learned. Let your child see that you, as an adult, keep learning new things; this instills an appreciation of learning as a lifelong process.

As the various hunting seasons approach (most of them occur in the fall), ask your child if he or she knows why hunting is restricted to short periods of the year in most places, and why certain animals, such as wolves, cannot be hunted. Such discussions offer a chance to talk about animals' life cycles, ecological balance, and the food chain.

The environment is part of the third grade curriculum. Ask your child about things we can do to ensure a healthy environment. See what he or she knows about air and water pollution, toxic wastes, soil erosion, and rain forest destruction.

Your child will be learning about germs and about ways to protect oneself from disease. Ask, "How are diseases spread?" Your might ask about colds, the chicken pox, measles, and the flu.

One important aspect of understanding newly learned material is being able to link it to other information, ideas, and concepts. Help your child practice making these connections. It often helps to "map" them out on a sheet of paper. For example, you might say, "Let's think of everything we can that relates to *feathers*." Write FEATHERS in the center of a sheet of paper. Then write down all the images and ideas you can think of and connect them with lines.

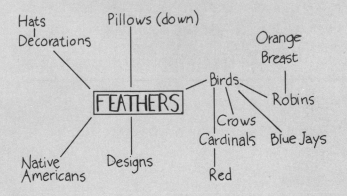

Try more exercises in making connections. You could start with ELECTRICITY. The related images and ideas might include currents, wires, lightning, batteries, nuclear energy, waterfalls, Benjamin Franklin, Thomas Edison, streetlights, plugs, light bulbs, sound, radio and television, and more. The larger the number of connections, the broader your child's understanding of the central concept.

Using old newspapers folded into corners or rolled into cylinders, construct buildings and towns together. See how high you can build a tower before it leans or falls. Discuss the features of the tallest structures—those that fell as well as those that stayed up.

Continue encouraging your child to examine his or her own learning. Ask, "How well do you understand the science you are learning in school? Is there anything you don't understand? What would you like to know more about?"

Social Studies

In the third grade, as in the earlier grades, the social studies relate principally to relationships within families and communities. The third grade curriculum increases the emphasis on geography and history, especially in relation to the local community. A child's work in social studies, as in the other subject areas, should be concrete and visible in the world. Many of the stories that are read to children, or that children read for themselves, have social studies themes.

Watch the television news together on occasion. Let the events on the news become a basis for conversation. You might also watch documentaries about historical figures with your child; biography is a good basis for helping children learn about history.

Look at photographs together. Family pictures showing you and your child at different ages are a good choice. Ask, "What can you remember about these earlier times? What is different now?"

Look at photographs of children in other parts of the world. See whether your child knows where these children come from, and then ask him or her to tell you about the different countries the children come from.

Social studies in the third grade includes learning more about maps and various regions of the world. You might ask your child what countries he or she knows about. Can your child find these countries on a globe or map?

Third graders study the globe. Ask your child to pick out the continents—Asia, Africa, South America, North America, Europe, Australia, Antarctica. Make a game of it, taking turns to find the continents. (You can do the same thing with the oceans.)

With a map or atlas, see if your child can use map coordinates (these are the guides maps have on the edges, usually numbers on one side and letters on another, rather than latitude and longitude).

Ask what scientists, carpenters, mechanics, lawyers, plumbers, physicians, and nurses do. Take turns thinking of various occupations, perhaps starting with people you know or characters in books.

Children celebrate several different holidays in school. Presidents' Day, Martin Luther King, Jr., Day, Veterans Day, Thanksgiving, and in some settings Cinco de Mayo receive the most attention. These celebrations are good opportunities to ask your child what he or she has learned about the presidents, Martin Luther King, Jr., and various national traditions.

Ask your child to share with you what he or she has learned about different ethnic and cultural groups in and around your community. What has your child learned about African Americans, Hispanics, Vietnamese, and Cambodians?

Ask your child to describe how a skyscraper is built, how a car is made, how wheat is harvested, how bread is made, how oil is carried from one part of the world to another, and so on. You will learn about your child's growing understanding of the world.

Look at maps of your town or city with your child. Using the map, ask your child how to get to various landmarks. Move from local to state maps. Take turns finding various cities and towns. Once you have found a town, ask your child how he or she would get there from home. How long might the trip take?

See if your child knows who the president of the United States is. How about the mayor of your town or city? The governor of your state? Ask what these persons do. You might also see what your child understands about the voting process.

Ask, "What Indian tribes do you know about?" "What do you know about them?"

Keep up the habit of asking your child, "What do you think?" about events and activities. Listen carefully to your child's responses. This tells you a great deal about what your child understands. It also tells your child that his or her opinions mean something.

Children at school tend to be concerned with fairness and taking responsibility. Find out what is expected of your child in class—for example, keeping the room orderly, making sure books are put back onto shelves, picking up paper, taking care of equipment or animals.

Problem solving is a vitally important skill. Get your child involved in the process of identifying problems and developing solutions. For example, you might ask, "What should we do? We need to decide where to plant a tree in our yard." Ask your child for suggestions and the reasons behind the suggestions. Share some of your own ideas. Together you can come up with a list of possible solutions.

A sense of history is important to ongoing learning. You might ask, "Do you know what our town (or city, or community) was like a hundred years ago? How did people travel then? How did they cook? How did they make a living? What was life like for children back then?"

Children hear a great deal about how we need to safeguard the environment and protect the world. Ask your child what he or she knows about pollution, recycling, and rain forests.

Engage in community service activities together. Work at a food shelter, or contribute time to various charities. Such activities are a chance to discuss the importance of service as part of citizenship.

Visit historical museums or sites together. During these visits, talk about how people lived in other times. What are the differences between past and present ways of life? What are the similarities?

Ask your child to teach you something he or she has learned in school.

Ask your child how his or her school could be better. What about the neighborhood? The city or town? What ideas does your child have for bringing about the suggested improvements?

Inquire about the rules at your child's school. What are they for? Are they necessary? See whether your child understands the relationship between those rules and the laws that govern our towns, cities, states, and nations.

Ask your child to give directions to the school, the park, the closest library, the supermarket. Are the directions accurate? Are they clear? If you did not already know the way, would you be able to find the places to which your child has directed you?

If you live in a city, ask your child what life is like in a small town. If you live in a small town, ask about life in a big city.

The United States is a land of immigrants. Make sure that you child knows where your family's ancestors came from; find the homeland(s) on a map. Ask your child about the backgrounds of other students in his or her class. What does your child know about recent immigrants from Mexico, the Caribbean, Southeast Asia, and Eastern Europe. Ask why so many people have come to this country and why people continue to come.

Work together on a chart or "map" of connections. You might start with MARTIN LUTHER KING, JR. The related ideas could include civil rights, nonviolence, "I have a dream," national holiday, African Americans, justice, the U.S. Constitution, desegregation, assassination, hero, and so on.

Various Native American peoples lived in the United States long before the Europeans came. Ask your child, "What Indian tribes lived in our area? How did they live?"

The news is full of struggles for freedom in various parts of the world. Inquire about your child's understanding of these events. Can he or she compare them with similar events in American history?

Offer as a starting point, "You have been learning about our community this year. What have you learned so far?" Periodically ask, "What new things have you learned about the community?"

Take walks through local cemeteries. Look for the oldest stones. Note how long people lived during various time periods, and the fact that many children died young (sometimes many in a single year, if there was an epidemic). Note also that names give clues to national origins. You can find links with history—perhaps people who were born or died in historic years such as 1865 or 1918.

Ask how many different countries are named on the front page of the day's newspaper.

Talk about recycling. How does it work in your community? Why is it important?

Plan a visit to an industrial plant—a good chance to see American industry at work. You will see how well your child understands how things are made. (Send for USA Plant Visits, Order #003-012-0041-7, Superintendent of Documents, U.S. Government Printing Office, Washington, DC, 20402. The document costs $2.80. You might suggest that your child write the letter of request.)

Ask your child, "How well do you understand the social studies you are learning in school? Is there anything you don't understand? What would you like to know more about?"

6 *Parents and Schools*

As I said in the introduction to this book, parents are critically important to their children's education. By reading to your children daily during the preschool and primary school years, including them in family conversations, listening to them, providing them with varied experiences, and understanding that play and the exploration of diverse objects and environments are vital elements of learning, you can contribute greatly to your children's development and help them become successful learners. Young children need the active interest of their parents. They need to see that their parents care about them and their learning. Furthermore, children should know that their parents value language and are inquisitive about the world—that their parents, in fact, are also learners.

As the elementary years proceed, it is crucial for parents to continue reading to their children, sharing interesting stories from the newspapers and magazines as well as from the rich literature of mythology, biography, and travel. They should take walks with their children, making note of the environment and posing interesting questions along the way. Playing board games that demand problem solving, or watching television and discussing the programs afterward, are also ways to share in a child's learning while fostering a healthy relationship.

As children get older and move through middle school and secondary school, their interactions with their parents necessarily change. But parents' support remains important. Parents will find that taking an interest in what their children are reading and writing is an excellent starting point for conversations, no matter what age the children are. They will also discover that they can learn a great deal from their adolescent children, who may be reading literature or studying historical and scientific topics that the parents either never knew or have forgotten.

The parents' partnership with the school is also important. Maintaining this partnership may seem easier and more natural when children are in the primary grades, but parents should consider it a priority throughout *all* the grades. In the best situations, teachers actively seek connections with parents. They call on the phone, write personal letters, and hold informal discussions. And they make certain that conferences are scheduled for times when parents are able to attend. If teachers do not do these things, then parents should ask *why*.

Parents should expect their children's teachers to explain fully what the school year will be like, what topics will be studied, what problems are to be explored, what is to be read, what kinds of writing will be done, how the teachers will assess their students' progress, and how parents will be kept informed. If this information is not made available to parents, the parents should ask for it regularly.

To make the most of whatever information teachers provide, parents should try to spend some time—a couple of days each year at a minimum—in their child's classroom, especially during the early years. This gives parents valuable direct insight into what their children's educational experiences are like. It also helps them understand the intentions of their children's teachers, which makes interactions between parents and teachers more constructive.

Many teachers actively encourage parents to be classroom partners. Parents may share some of their own experiences, read to children, take small groups of children on field trips, and the like. A few hours each week for such participation is very useful to both parents and their children.

How should parents approach their children's teachers and the schools? In most cases the teacher-parent exchange will be relatively easy. Teachers *want* connections with parents. They understand well the importance of parents as first and ongoing educators of their children. But they also know that parents have not always been sufficiently involved with their children or particularly responsive to teachers' efforts to interact with them. Both parents and teachers must strive for constructive, reciprocal exchanges.

Parents know their children. They know their interests and preferences, how they approach new situations, and how much they understand of the world. Parents need to share this knowledge with teachers in order to help the teachers be more effective. If your son or daughter is unhappy with school, feels unsuccessful or bored, seems not to be making progress as a learner, or is unable to take part in many of the conversations outlined in chapter 5, make an appointment with the child's teacher. *This is an important first step.*

Your meeting with the teacher should not be confrontational or angry. There is no need for defensiveness or anxiety. Share your concerns in as natural a manner as possible. If you have sensed that your child is unhappy about school, the teacher has probably sensed this also. If you have noticed that your child has lost interest in reading, seems uninquisitive about the natural world, or appears vague about mathematics and its uses, the teacher has probably observed these attitudes too. Now is the time for you and the teacher to come together on behalf of the child. Together, parents and teachers can figure out how to proceed. You might ask how you can be more helpful. Can the teacher suggest ways for you to enlarge your child's understanding of math, science, or language? Also inquire about what the teacher will do. Establish a schedule for meeting again to determine what progress is being made, and *keep* the schedule. If you create and maintain a seriousness of purpose where your child's education is concerned, you have taken a vital step toward improving the child's education.

As I said at the beginning, this book is intended to bring parents, children, and teachers together in a productive exchange centered on school learning. Most children, being the natural learners they are, will make academic progress in school—but their progress will be far greater if their parents are actively involved.

The schools generally meet students' needs reasonably well, if not always well enough. But they will also do far better if parents join with teachers in an active partnership. Chapter 1 of this book describes some of the qualities of a healthy school learning environment. An active partnership between parents and schools is necessary if such environments are to become the reality in all schools. Teachers should be supported in their desire for smaller classes in the early years, for a wide range of instructional materials, for strong arts programs. By providing such support, parents benefit their children and all children.

Appendix

Books Parents Might Find Useful

Armstrong, Thomas. *Awakening Your Child's Natural Genius.* Los Angeles: J. P. Tarcher, 1987.

———. *In Their Own Way: Discovery and Encouraging Your Child's Personal Learning Style.* Los Angeles: J. P. Tarcher, 1987.

Bissex, Glenda. *Gnys at Wrk: A Child Learns to Write and Read.* Cambridge: Harvard University Press, 1980.

Burns, Marilyn. *The I Hate Mathematics! Book.* Boston: Little, Brown, 1975.

Caulkins, Lucy M. *Lessons from a Child.* Portsmouth, NH: Heinemann, 1986.

Children's Television Workshop Parents' Guide to Learning. *Kids Who Love to Learn.* New York: Prentice Hall, 1989.

Clay, Marie. *Writing Begins at Home.* Portsmouth, NH: Heinemann, 1987.

Gardner, Howard. *Frames of Mind: The Theory of Multiple Intelligence.* New York: Basic Books, 1983.

Goodlad, John I. *A Place Called School.* New York: McGraw-Hill, 1987.

Healy, Jane. *Your Child's Growing Mind: A Parent's Guide to Learning from Birth to Adolescence.* New York: Doubleday, 1987.

Kline, Peter. *The Everyday Genius: Restoring Children's Natural Joy of Learning.* Arlington, VA: Great Ocean, 1988.

Lappe, Frances Moore. *What To Do After You Turn Off the TV.* New York: Ballantine, 1985.

Maeroff, Gene. *The School-Smart Parent*. New York: Random House, 1989.

Papert, Seymour. *Mindstorms: Children, Computers, and Powerful Ideas*. New York: Basic Books, 1980.

Rosner, Jerome. *Helping Children Overcome Learning Difficulties*. New York: Walker, 1979.

Schimmels, Cliff. *How To Help Your Child Survive and Thrive in Public Schools*. New York: Revell, 1982.

Schon, Isabel. *Books in Spanish for Children and Young Adults*. Metuchen, NJ: Scarecrow Press, 1985.

Singer, Dorothy, et al. *Use TV to Your Child's Advantage: The Parent's Guide*. Washington, DC: Acropolis, 1990.

Stein, Sara. *The Science Book*. Boston: Little, Brown, 1975.

Taylor, Denny. *Family Literacy: Young Children Learning to Read and Write*. Portsmouth, NH: Heinemann, 1983.

Weitzman, David. *My Backyard History Book*. Boston: Little, Brown, 1975.

Wilms, Denise, and Ilene Cooper. *A Guide to Non-Sexist Children's Books*. Chicago: Academy, 1987.

Several Guides to Good Literature for Elementary School–Age Children

American Library Association. *Opening Doors for Pre-School Children and Their Parents*. Washington, DC: American Library Association, 1981.

Jett-Simpson, May, ed. *Adventuring with Books*. Urbana, IL: National Council of Teachers of English, 1989.

Lamme, Linda. *Growing Up Reading: Sharing with Your Child the Joys of Reading.* Washington, DC: Acropolis, 1985.

Lipson, Eden Ross. *The New York Times Parent's Guide to the Best Books for Children.* New York: Times Books, 1991.

Lorrick, Nancy. *A Parent's Guide to Children's Reading.* New York: Bantam, 1982.

Pollock, Barbara. *The Black Experience in Children's Books.* New York: New York Public Libraries, 1984.

Booklists

Each Spring, *Booklist*, the journal of the American Library Association, publishes a list of notable books for children, based on "literary quality, originality of text and illustrations, design, format, subject matter of interest to children, and likelihood of acceptance by children."

The Fall issue of *The Reading Teacher*, published by the International Reading Association, lists books children themselves select each year as "best books." (Available at no charge by sending a stamped, self-addressed #10 envelope to the Children's Book Council, 67 Irving Place, New York, NY 10003.)

The Spring issue of *Social Education*, published by the National Council of the Social Studies, lists books selected each year that "are written primarily for children . . . ; emphasize human relations; present an original theme." (Available at no charge by sending a stamped, self-addressed #10 envelope to the Children's Book Council, 67 Irving Place, New York, NY 10003.)

The Spring issue of *Science and Children*, the journal of the National Science Teachers Association, lists children's books selected annually for readability and science accuracy and interest. (Available at no charge by sending a stamped, self-addressed #10 envelope to the Children's Book Council, 67 Irving Place, New York, NY 10003).

VITO PERRONE is Director of Teacher Education and Chair of Teaching, Curriculum, and Learning Environments at Harvard University. He has previous experience as a public school teacher, a university professor of history, education, and peace studies (University of North Dakota), and as dean of the New School and the Center for Teaching and Learning (both at the University of North Dakota). Dr. Perrone has written extensively about such issues as educational equity, humanities curriculum, progressive education, and evaluation. His most recent books are: *A Letter to Teachers: Reflections on Schooling and the Art of Teaching*; *Enlarging Student Assessment in Schools*; *Working Papers: Reflections on Teachers, Schools, and Communities*; *Visions of Peace*; and *Johanna Knudsen Miller: A Pioneer Teacher*.